A Cel

Little Inst

GW00789987

A Celebrity's
Little Instruction Book

**JASMINE BIRTLES
& MARC BLAKE**

B⊞XTREE

First published 2001 by Boxtree
an imprint of Pan Macmillan Ltd
Pan Macmillan, 20 New Wharf Road, London N1 9RR
Basingstoke and Oxford
Associated companies throughout the world
www.panmacmillan.com

ISBN 0 7522 6152 5

1 3 5 7 9 8 6 4 2

A CIP catalogue record for this book is available from the British Library.

Design by Dan Newman/Perfect Bound Ltd
Printed by The Bath Press Ltd, Bath

Oh the roar of the greasepaint! The smell of the crowd! No wonder so many of us want to be famous – and let's face it, it's getting easier every day. You don't need talent, looks, intelligence or even a personality now, merely an overwhelming desire to be noticed in the street and a willingness to make a complete arse of yourself in front of the cameras. So if you want to be like the kids from *Fame* take note of the words of wisdom in this tome which has been written by the priest and priestess of the new cult of Celebrity. Obey their commandments and you will gain immortality – or at least a couple of paragraphs on Page 3.

If at first you don't succeed, tell everyone you did.

Celeb definitions:

A-list – they throw a party for you

B-list – you get a VIP invite to A-list parties

C-list – you blag your way into B-list parties

D-list – you end up in the corner at parties with Christopher Biggins or Sue Pollard

E-list – you *are* Christopher Biggins or Sue Pollard

The problem with Hollywood is they shoot too many films and not enough actors.

The secret of news reading is to sound sincere. If you can fake that, you're made.

You know you're not famous if your name is so low on the programme you're asked to quote for printing.

Soap actor necessities: a miserable-looking face, one tabloid-friendly vice and a solid refusal to do any actual acting.

Game shows – the discovery of artificial life.

Page Three model: body by Barbie, brains by MFI.

Charity begins at home, so do a benefit concert to pay for your conservatory.

Never gossip. It's rude and it takes people's minds off you.

What does a rock star have
that gets bigger if you stroke it?
His ego.

The best actors at an awards ceremony
are the good losers.

13

Make sure everyone in a lift knows you're a star by admiring yourself in the mirrors, refusing to press the buttons, and constantly asking, 'Are we at the penthouse yet?'

   14

If Kirk Douglas is tipped to star in a movie about
your life it may be time for a facelift.

   15

Don't believe your own hype – S-Club 7 are still being sued over their hit single 'There ain't no party like an S-Club party' because, technically, there is and McDonalds also throw in a free Happy Meal.

   16

There are several ways of staying famous;
unfortunately most of them involve building a time
machine or sleeping with a plastic surgeon.

Celebrity algebra: in order to calculate the exact
value of pi, simply try to separate Marlon Brando
from the dish.

What's the difference between
an agent and a toilet seat? A toilet seat only has to
deal with one arsehole at a time.

Celebrity maths:

if Johnny Depp travels towards Hollywood at a speed of 6 miles per day and Brad Pitt leaves from the same point two days later at a speed of 30 m.p.h., how long will it take Robert Downey Jnr to overtake them both on his imaginary crack-powered jet-cycle?

You know the model diet's getting out of hand when Kate Moss sends you food parcels, and you have to jump around under the shower to get wet.

   20

FAME = Forget Art, Money's Everything.

If there's no business like showbusiness, how come 90 per cent of actors never do any bloody work?

The more money you have
the more things you get given for free.

The shortest distance between two rock stars
is a groupie.

  22

STAR = Stop Trying, All Right?

How many celebrities does it take
to change a lightbulb?
Listen, guys, for the last time –
will you get away from my light!

Real stars aren't worried about the size of their egos.
What's important is the size of the trailer!

Don't appear in any movie where your name
features lower down on the poster
than the stunt horse.

   24

How to spot a celebrity in a supermarket:
she's the one shoplifting from the organic counter.

Don't bother with religion.
Why search for a Supreme Being when
Stephen Spielberg is in the phonebook?

   25

How to spot a celebrity in McDonald's:
he's the one asking for the à la carte menu.

How to know when you've made it:
Robbie Williams denies having sex with you but
Chris Evans is not ruling it out.

   26

Being a child star means you owe everything
to your parents, even though you've got a
restraining order against them.

Why did the groupie cross the road?
Because she was under a court order to stay
500 yards from the chicken.

Celebrity tribute songs:
'Come Die With Me' (Frank Sinatra),
'I'll Be Mulch for Christmas' (John Denver),
'Don't Go Breaking My Neck' (Rod Hull and Emu).

Celebrity nicknames:
'The Phallus from Dallas' (Patrick Duffy),
'The Sinner from Pinner' (Jane March),
'The Porridge from Norwich' (Vanessa Feltz).

Celebrity drink: dry Martini, shaken not stirred.
Wannabe drink: rum and coke.
Has-been drink: Toilet Duck with a meths chaser.

Do adopt some sort of religion but
only if it involves interesting costumes and exotic
rituals and doesn't demand any actual morality.
Catholicism, for example.

Use your fame to speak out on political issues.
Nelson Mandela may have overcome apartheid, but
could he have touched a billion disturbed
schoolboys without the help of the Spice Girls?

Being a heroic failure can often bring you fame. If you can't be heroic just being loud will do.

The average celebrity has a shorter shelf life than yoghurt, and less culture.

Learn how to age gracefully. We can't all look as marvellous as Peter Stringfellow.

Celebrity marriages may be short-lived but alimony lasts for ever.

It's getting harder to be cool. In the sixties the Rolling Stones made it by pissing in a garage forecourt. Now you could piss on Keith Richards, except he's probably done it already.

   35

Don't expose too much of yourself.
This is known as the Keith Chegwin Syndrome.
It's not clever, and in Keith's case
it's certainly not big.

Don't go around espousing serious political views.
Tony Blair doesn't bother, so why should you?

Watch who you screw on the way up.
You could get screwed by them on your way down.

   37

There's no such thing as bad publicity –
unless you're Gary Glitter.

If you fail in your career and feel overwhelmed
with bitterness, don't despair. You can always
become a journalist.

If you want to get away from it all and go where no one will notice you, just host your own show on Channel 5.

Regularly complain about press intrusion in as many newspapers, magazines, TV and radio programmes as you can.

   39

Docusoaps: made by the cynical, filled with the ordinary, watched by the brain-dead.

Have different stage names for your various jobs. It'll piss off journalists and confuse the Inland Revenue.

All celebrities are whores. Although it's best not to mention this during the interview.

On your way up you'll have to be nice to people you don't like. Try practising with your family.

Don't let money be your only motivation. Revenge is a good one too.

Be like Richard Branson. Develop an ego like a barrage balloon and then sail it round the world.

   42

Many people in showbusiness have worked their way up from the bottom. Especially rent-boys.

For many starlets their first real job is a blowjob, quickly dispelling the myth that it's better to give than receive.

   43

If the public love you for being crap, be happy to be crap. Welcome to Digital TV.

Paparazzi can be a problem. Make sure your agent tips them off where you are.

Never apologize to anyone. You'll be hated by production staff but loved by the suits. And who's paying your fee?

You know you're losing your movie-star looks when you're the centre-spread of *Horse and Hound*.

   45

If you're wondering what kind of pop star to become, remember that your average Wild Man of Rock gets to trash hotel bedrooms, snort every substance known to man and bed women like Angelina Jolie while looking no better than a lanky tattooed testicle on legs. You work it out.

   46

Never put off till tomorrow what the plastic surgeon can do today.

Don't put all your eggs in one basket – or if you do, don't give the basket to your agent.

Laugh and the world laughs with you,
cry and you'll be on *EastEnders* before you know it.

An apple a day is more than
the average supermodel eats in a week.

If at first you don't succeed – pray for a sequel.

Fame is a fickle mistress, which must make
Amanda Holden very famous indeed.

   49

A good celebrity PR will separate fact from fiction,
and then dish out the fiction.

The ideal situation is to make vast amounts of
money for doing nothing. But we can't all be
members of the Royal Family.

It's vital to keep up with the latest trends in designer drugs – to be a 'medicated follower of fashion'.

Having a famous husband can make you a celeb – particularly if he's someone else's.

   51

The Priory is the place for celebrity nervous breakdowns – it's the size of their bills that does it.

Time was when having sex with a politician could get you into the papers. Now you have to have sex with a politician's dog to get any press interest.

Marrying royalty may be an easy way to fame but who wants to be a Queen with no dress sense? Mind you, it never did Boy George any harm.

   53

Never call yourself a groupie – you are simply a *very* personal assistant.

Actresses ask, 'Am I willing to get out of bed for that sort of money?' Porn stars ask, 'Am I willing to get into bed for that sort of money?'

Becoming a celeb is not about talent but about
persistence so don't take no for an answer,
even when the restraining order kicks in.

When posing for 'society' photos, try to look as vacant and drunk as possible. That way the photo is guaranteed to get into the magazine.

Celebs can get away with any sin including murder, rape and drug pushing. Even terminal dullness will get you a place on *Big Brother*.

No musical skills, coordination or ability to say any real words other than 'in the house'?
Great – be a club DJ.

Celebrity marriages come in three sizes,
short, long and Elizabeth Taylor.

Words every pop star dreads: 'You might not have
any fans here, but hey, you're big in Germany!'

Radio DJ career:
young Turk on pirate radio station,
go-getter on local hip station,
drive-time show on Radio 1,
chatty talk-show on Radio 5,
2 a.m. graveyard slot on Radio Quiet.

The top celeb fabrics are silk, velvet and rubber.
Never bother with black plastic unless you are a
Tory MP with a penchant for oranges.

Supermodel girlfriends are for photo-opportunities,
not sex. At under seven stone they can shatter
if jostled.

Celebrity maths: the bigger the column inches
the smaller the talent.

Good way to leave a nightclub: with a supermodel, in a limo. Bad way to leave a nightclub: with a can of Tennant's Super, in a wheelie-bin.

  62

Essentials for the airport VIP lounge:
shades, baby, Louis Vuitton luggage,
twenty-four condoms filled with heroin in stomach.

Celebrity maths:
for every hyphen in the surname,
deduct fifty IQ points.

   63

How to tell if you're tired of being a celeb –
the fridge light goes on and you don't do twenty
minutes; you stop wearing sunglasses indoors;
you won't even sign for a parcel.

The best time to make a celebrity comeback: after you're dead.

You know your celebrity cred has reached its sell-by date when . . . you open a supermarket on a wet Thursday, in Norfolk, drunk, with Christopher Biggins.

   65

You know you're a celeb when . . . there are paparazzi
in your fridge; someone's going through your bins
and it's not a fox; Patsy Kensit wants to marry you.

Jobs that will never achieve celebrity status: embalmer, taxidermist, farmer, proctologist, proctologist/farmer.

Actual knowledge will hinder a TV interview. Real experts are those you leech off to further your career.

How to spot the child of a celeb: designer romper suit, tinted windows in the buggy, first words are, 'Mummy's in rehab.'

Where to be seen: Met bar. Harrods.
Where not to be seen: Metropolitan line. Harvester.

Celebrity mottoes:
'Marry in *Hello*, repent at the lawyers.'

Famous for fifteen minutes,
desperate for the rest of your life.

A-list stalker: a psychopathic obsessive who tries to kill a president. E-list stalker: Richard and Judy fan who tries to kidnap Alan Titchmarsh.

Celeb illnesses explained: flu –drunk; kidney infection – drunk; food poisoning – drunk, stoned, can't be arsed to get out of bed.

   70

Kids' TV presenter's job description:
young, attractive, constantly hyperactive –
or willing to drink fifteen pints of Sunny Delight
and snort seven grams of coke daily.

It's time to go into detox when ... you're constantly mistaken for Oliver Reed; and you're a woman.

You know you've made it when your hairstyle beats you at the Oscars.

It's time to come off that painful diet when ...
Kate Moss says you're looking thin;
you slip between the cracks of your sanded-down
floorboards and end up in the cellar;
you can play a tune on your ribs.

You know you've had too much cocaine when . . .
every time you go to the loo you instantly lick the
top of the cistern.

A true celebrity is not two-faced.
They have at least five.

The best thing about being a celeb is the freebies:
free clothes, free make-up, free-basing.

Ruin a celebrity chef's day. Tell him 'it's just cooking'.
Ditto for gardening.

   75

You know you've made it when ...
young women approach you for sex;
other celebrities are envious of you;
Prince William wants your autograph.

You know you haven't made it when . . .
young women approach you with a can of Mace;
your mum is envious of you;
Prince Edward wants your autograph.

You know you've made it when the only thing
in your life that hasn't been profiled in the
Sunday Times is your dog. Yet.

You know it's all over when ... there are people less famous than you in the 'where are they now?' slots; you open a supermarket and the old ladies accuse you of pushing in; your perma-tan makes you look more like the Tango Man.

You can live on promise until you're twenty-five.
After that it's Prozac.

When a celeb says she's getting a new pair of
trainers they'll be called Jorg and Karl
and have six-pack stomachs.

The ideal male celebrity: brains of Stephen Fry,
body of Peter Andre, grace of David Beckham.
Non-ideal celeb: brains of David Beckham,
body of Stephen Fry, grace of Peter Andre.

A celebrity's ideal weight? Darling, we never wait!

Definition of a supermodel: cannot lift a small poodle, but can lift a packet of cigarettes, shoplift a Cartier watch and will one day have three facelifts.

Celebrity sound bites you'll never hear. 'I just got this great part in a made-for-TV movie!' 'No, I have no projects coming up. I'm unemployed.' 'I hate charity.' 'He was hell to work with. A complete cunt.'

Celebrity bisexuality – the perfect way to ensure a date on New Year's Eve.

What to demand of your hotel: cacti, urine, special Vulcan diet, another hotel.

Products you should endorse: perfume; exercise videos, designer clothes. Products you should not endorse: foot plasters, porn videos, Oxfam clothes.

If all else fails – out yourself as a closet heterosexual.

85

When holidaying with a mystery lover, take only
essentials: thong, sun cream and paparazzi.

Remember, dressing down means slobbing it
in $1,000 worth of designer gear, not a shell suit
and a McDonald's.

Celebrity homes must always look like an art gallery: exclusive, surrounded by guards and full of expensive rubbish.

When you kiss and tell, ensure that all heavy objects are stowed away, like lawyers.

   87

Three marriages are fine. Any more and it looks like you're buying people.

Celebrity mums, you may have just given birth but that's no excuse for not getting back into a crop top inside a week.

Poverty chic does not mean Artex walls,
horse brasses and the Pound Shop.
That's how people in Lancashire actually live.

Exotic celebrity holiday destinations
where you can guarantee to escape the crowds:
Alaska, Guam, Bradford.

'I'd give away my six-million-dollar-a-movie fee,
but my agent won't let me.'

It's not what you know, it's who you screw.

Celebrities ought to have a beach place in the
Hamptons. Littlehampton won't do.

Name your baby after your therapist.
That's where it'll end up anyway.

Always turn down the first offer, even if it's emergency surgery.

Weimaraner, chinchilla, Dalmatian. Never get a pet whose breed you can pronounce.

Don't ever worry about being taken seriously.
Someone will always drag up that old 1980s
outfit/job/ex-lover/embarrassing political coup.

   93

Always arrive late and leave early.
That way you'll never eat any food.

You know you've made it when someone mentions
Malibu and you think of home – not getting pissed
with the girls in 'Ibeefa'.

Good places to be smuggled out of:
Mount Sinai Hospital, Harley Street clinics.
Bad places to be smuggled out of:
St Mary's Genito-Urinary Clinic, prisons.

Doesn't *mystery blonde* sound better than
adulterous bitch?

A perfect celebrity couple is one where both
partners manage to keep their infidelity a secret
for more than two years.

Clothing guide for female celebs:
the less you wear, the more the coverage.

How to tell a celebrity's true age:
take the age they give you and add on the number
of marriages and facelifts.

Sex symbol = masturbation aid.

Are you a vacuous hypocritical compulsive liar?
You're on your way.

  98

Botox injections will freeze your expression for years.
Try not to have it done at the same time
as they give you the bill.

Celebrity bad behaviour is expected.
Imagine you are a three-year-old. Or Liam Gallagher.

   99

Never dish the dirt yourself, that's what 'friends',
'spokesmen' and 'Palace insiders' are for.

Forget Yoga, Pilates and Alexander Technique, the
only real fitness regime is dysentery and a drill
sergeant.

Celebrities fear only three things: physical danger,
anonymity and carbohydrates.

Forget expensive anniversary presents.
A liposuction voucher says it all.

  101

If your agent isn't returning your calls, don't worry,
he's probably misplaced something –
like your career.

If your ghostwritten autobiography doesn't hit the
bestseller lists, then a reviewer has probably read it.

If your film tanks in the first weekend,
blame the director ... who will blame the studio ...
who will blame the writer ... who will blame you.
What do you care?

The last person to turn to is your hairdresser –
who else will continue to lie so convincingly?

Everyone loves celebrity. Keep saying that until
you meet your stalker.

  104

Treat your body like a temple.
Keep it empty and don't let anyone in.

You cannot go wrong with black leather –
unless it's being worn by the arresting officer.

   105

Starlets: remember, there's no longer any need to buy a dress for the film premiere. A hankie will do.

Acceptance speeches should be like children, short and hysterical.

An exclusive interview is what you give
to each journalist for fifteen minutes,
twenty-five times a day.

Don't just have a sprog by some guy you met in a bar. 'Exclusively reveal' to the papers your 'secret love child' by a 'mystery lover' and rake in the cash. You really aren't getting the hang of it yet, are you?

Cover up your family history and get sympathy at the same time by claiming you were an orphan.

Celebrity is the gap between wannabe and has-been.

  109

In awards ceremonies, always thank your parents.
They may still have some incriminating photos.

   110

Cool: stretch limo. Uncool: stretch marks.

Cool: black Raybans. Uncool: black eyes.

Porn actress maths:
twenty blowjobs = one nose job.

Emotions you will no longer require as a celebrity:
humility, self-awareness, shame.

Real love is always closer than you think –
sometimes only as far away as a mirror.

Celebrity nightmare: economy class.

If you still think Groucho is one of the Marx brothers, you really haven't been paying attention.

In the future everyone will be famous for being famous for fifteen minutes.

Beauty makes its own rules, the first one being
'don't touch' – unless you're being well paid for that
gratuitous sex scene.

  115

Confession is good for the soul –
and the bank balance.

  116

Celebrity egos come in three sizes,
blimp, zeppelin and Feltz.

Aspire to appear on the cover of
Vogue, Vanity Fair and *Heat.*
Not *Readers' Wives, Big Jugs Monthly* or *Puzzler.*

When doing charity work in Africa,
try not to ask the locals for the secret of how they
got so wonderfully thin.

If all else fails, killing another celeb
will guarantee you celebrity.

Choose your pop persona carefully.
A Bad-Ass Rapper can be misogynist, homophobic and even incontinent.
A Boy Next Door Ballad Singer, however, has to be nice to girls, have good teeth and eventually come out of the closet with his gay lover.

If the BBC does a 'season' of your films
you're either a classic actor or dead.

The Oscars: a vehicle for recognizing the talents of
the world's top dress designers.

   120

Top celebrity status:
Hermès names a handbag after you.
Bottom celebrity status:
Boots names a surgical support after you.

Celebrity nudity:
A-list star, you have a stunt bottom for love scenes;
B-list star, you'll show your own bottom in love
scenes; E-list star, you *are* the stunt bottom in love
scenes.

You know you've had too many facelifts when . . .
Michael Jackson starts looking normal to you.

   123

Products to endorse: Versace. Products not to endorse: verruca plasters.

When you kiss and tell, make sure you've told your family and kissed them goodbye.

Make sure you only do charity work for people who will make you look really good on the TV reports.

Money makes the world go round,
but it cannot reverse time.

Getting friendly with the press is like wandering into
a lion's den covered in barbecue sauce.

Celebrity rhyming slang:
Give us a Zoe (Ball) = call
You're having a Steffi (Graff)= laugh
What a load of Emmerdale (Farm) = bollocks

Jasmine Birtles has had a glittering career in showbusiness. She started as a stripper for the blind and in her early twenties worked as a lap-dancer for the Faculty and Institute of Actuaries. A great beauty, she was painted by David Hockney, from head to toe in 'Warm Toast' vinyl matt. She has modelled, mostly in clay but occasionally in butter, and is currently manager of a troop of travelling valuations officers who visit seaside towns setting up ad-hoc valuations and structural surveying performances. She is the only surviving member of the Romanov family – or at least she is until the drugs wear off.

Marc Blake is a celebrity in his own lunchtime. A veteran of swanky Soho watering holes, there is no bar from which he has not been ejected. So addicted is he to publicity that he purposefully drives at 90 m.p.h. so that he can smile for the speed cameras. He is also a habitué, a roué and other French words that lose something in translation. He is currently appearing in an off-off-Fringe production of *Oklahimie*, by the Dyslexic Players. His last words were 'Now, how does this thing . . . ? BANG.'